Using Numbers at Work

by Cathy French

I am a grocer.
I am using numbers
at work.

3

I am a builder.
I am using numbers
at work.

5

I am a doctor.
I am using numbers
at work.

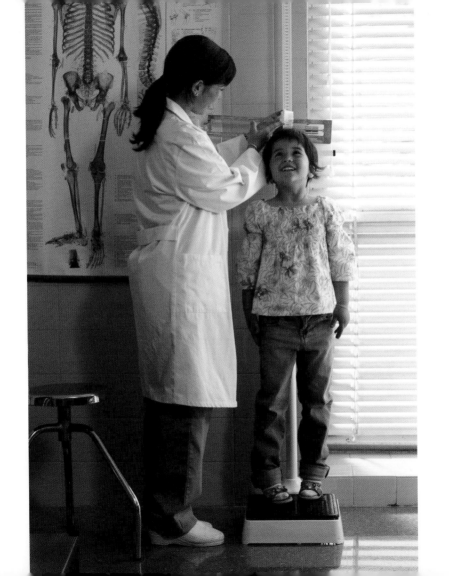

7

I am a cook.
I am using numbers
at work.

I am a librarian.
I am using numbers
at work.

I am an umpire.
I am using numbers
at work.

13

I am a teller.
I am using numbers
at work.

I am using numbers, too.